Styling
Spaces

Discover your unique room
style with quizzes, activities,
crafts—and more!

by Carrie Anton
illustrated by Marilena Perilli
and Flávia Conley

Published by American Girl Publishing

16 17 18 19 20 21 22 LEO 10 9 8 7 6 5 4 3 2 1

Editorial Development: Carrie Anton, Emily Osborn
Art Direction and Design: Gretchen Becker
Production: Jeannette Bailey, Laura Markowitz, Cynthia Stiles, Kristi Tabrizi
Photography: Radlund Photography, Derek Brabender
Craft Stylist: Carrie Anton
Set Stylist: Emily Osborn
Wardrobe Stylist: Aubre Andrus
Hair Stylist: Lynée Ruiz
Doll Stylist: Jane Amini
Illustrations: Marilena Perilli, Flávia Conley

Stock Photography: page 22 (mirror sphere), © iStock.com/opolja; page 22 (stopwatch), © iStock.com/s-cphoto; page 22 (wastepaper basket), © iStock.com/humbak; page 28 (watercolor sun), © iStock.com/anamad; page 28 (flowers), © iStock.com/kotoffei; page 28 (hand-drawn typography poster), © iStock.com/Afavete; page 28 (tree), © iStock.com/ririe777; page 28 (butterfly photo), © iStock.com/BalazsKovacs; page 28 (girl on unicorn), © iStock.com/rilora; page 28 (french bulldog), © iStock.com/Toru-Sanogawa; page 29 (giant panda), © iStock.com/VanWyckExpress; page 34 (floral heart), © iStock.com/Kumer; page 34 (hand-drawn typography poster), © iStock.com/Afavete.

americangirl.com/service

Dear Reader,

Your bedroom is more than just a place to sleep. It's where you go to be alone, do your homework, or hang out with your friends. It's the place that is home to all of your favorite things—the stuffed animal you've had since you were a baby, your diary filled with secret wishes and private thoughts, and photos capturing favorite memories spent with family and friends. It's your own space to dream, learn, and grow. Your room is the best place for you to be yourself, so it only makes sense that it should reflect a style that is as unique as you are.

To transform your room into your ideal space, turn the pages and open the door to a whole new place! We've filled the pages of this book with activities, crafts, and tear-outs that will help you add some simple touches to your space. The ideas in this book offer easy ways to make big changes so that in the end, you'll create a room filled with your personal style.

Your friends at American Girl

 When you see this symbol, it means you need an adult to help you with all or part of the task. ALWAYS ask for help before continuing. Ask an adult to approve all craft supplies before you use them—some are not safe for kids. When creating doll crafts, remember that dyes from supplies may bleed onto your doll or her clothes and leave permanent stains. Use lighter colors when possible, and check your doll often to make sure the colors aren't transferring to her body, her vinyl, or her clothes. And never get your doll wet! Water and heat increase dye rub-off.

Creativity
is intelligence
having fun.

Room for Style

Which theme is perfect for your personal space?

Sometimes following a theme is the best place to start when transforming your space. Choose the answers that describe you best to see which design direction your room should follow.

1. Your dream vacation would be . . .

a. shopping in Paris.

b. an African safari.

c. hiking the Grand Canyon.

d. surfing the Hawaiian waves.

e. touring the sights of New York City.

2. If you could have any animal as a pet, which one would you choose?

a. a cute little dog

b. a spotted giraffe

c. a fast horse

d. a colorful parrot

e. a purr-fect cat

3. Rise and shine—it's breakfast time. What's to eat?

a. croissants and tea

b. sweet monkey bread and elephant ear pastries

c. crunchy granola sprinkled over wildberry yogurt

d. a pineapple-mango smoothie

e. bagel and cream cheese to go

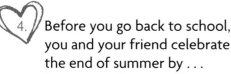

4. Before you go back to school, you and your friend celebrate the end of summer by . . .

a. buying matching sparkly bracelets at the mall.

b. visiting your favorite animals at the petting zoo.

c. pitching a backyard tent and eating s'mores.

d. spending an entire day at the beach.

e. catching the new movie based on your favorite book.

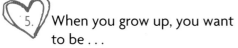

5. When you grow up, you want to be . . .

a. a fashion designer.

b. a veterinarian.

c. a park ranger.

d. a marine biologist.

e. a writer.

6. Which top would most likely be in your closet?

a.

b.

c.

d.

e.

7. Most of the pics you take are of . . .

a. new outfits you put together from unique vintage store finds.

b. your pets. They're just so funny and easy to photograph!

c. birds, butterflies, and leaves that fall from trees.

d. anything beachy—it reminds you of a vacation!

e. big buildings and colorful graffiti.

Paris Pretty

If you answered mostly a's, then it's a boutique chic room for you! Can't jet-set to France anytime soon? No worries! Transform your space to look like it's straight out of a Paris postcard. Mix girly colors—such as pinks, purples, or teals—with bold black and white for the perfect color palette. Add ruffled edges, a mini chandelier, and lots of soft pillows for room decor that says *ooh la la*!

Sassy Safari

If you answered mostly b's, adventure awaits in your very own bedroom! Animals and the outdoors are what make you wild, so of course they'll fit right in as fantastic flair for your decorated space. Mix and match neutral-color animal prints with a bold color to really stand out from the pack. Explore ways to add different textures, just like you'd experience in the bush, and your room is sure to go in the right direction.

Happy Camper

If you answered mostly c's, look for ways to bring the outdoors in! You prefer to be snuggled in your sleeping bag while gazing up at the stars as you drift off to dreamland. Just because you have a ceiling above doesn't mean you can't turn a night-light or glow-in-the-dark decals into your own indoor star show. Add plaid and woodsy touches to your space and be on the lookout for lantern-style lamps. Make more of your floor by setting up cushions similar to sitting around the campfire.

Beauty and the Beach

If you answered mostly d's, surf's up! Set the scene for your space
using sun, sand, and ocean waves as wonderful inspiration. Decorate
the edges of a frame with seashells you found at the beach; then add
in a picture of the biggest sandcastle you ever built. Use clean sand
buckets to store hair accessories, pens, pencils, and other loose odds
and ends. Keep the colors light and airy, or turn up the heat with
accents of teal, fuchsia, and bright yellow.

City Slick

If you answered mostly e's, the urban scene is the ultimate theme for your space. Cities are spectacular with bright lights, tall buildings, and unique sights around every corner. Make your room feel just as bold by mixing in different metal textures with bright colors. If there's something specific that you love about downtown—the music, the food, the museums, or the art—add it to your place to make this style more customized to your interests.

Design
Dreams

At this interior-design party for four, gather together to change your rooms from boring to bright all in one night!

Sure, you could decorate your room all on your own, but when it comes to being creative, four heads are better than one! Invite your friends over for a design party that starts with studio time and ends with new statement pieces to spruce up your space.

Design Studio

Create a "studio" where you and your fellow interior designers can dream and draw. Cover a table with a roll of craft paper (found at craft stores), and set up each workstation with colored pencils, inspiring pictures, and color swatches. Encourage girls to draw on the "tablecloth" or use it to jot down lists of ideas for your dream room decor.

Paint Chip Banner

Turn your parents' leftover paint chip sample cards (free at home improvement stores, but be mindful that you don't take too many) into a colorful banner. Cut the cards into triangles. Punch a hole into the top two corners of six different cards. String ribbon through the holes, and knot as you go to keep the cards from slipping. Add a decorative chipboard letter to each, spelling out the word "Create." Hang it in the "studio."

Favors

Door Decor and More

Thank your friends for sharing their creativity with gifts they can take home and use in their own rooms. For each girl, fill a mini plastic paint can (found at craft stores) with a small sketchpad, colored pencils, markers, fabric swatches, and paint chips to inspire design ideas. Include one of the door hangers from the back of the book that she can fill in to match her room perfectly.

Game

Musical Collage

Ask your mom, dad, or sibling to play DJ for this game. Set up some music that is easy to stop and start. Lay out four small blank poster boards around a table. In the center of the table, place old magazines and catalogues, craft supplies such as scissors, crayons, and glue, and various decorative items, such as ribbons, stickers, buttons, and rhinestones. Each girl starts by standing in front of a poster board. When the music starts, each girl begins to decorate. When the music stops, everyone walks around the table to the right. When the music starts again, each girl has to add to the poster board that is in front of her. Keep going until the collages are complete. Send each girl home with the art she finished so that she can display it in her space.

Food

Colorful Cookies

Surprise guests with cookies that look just like paint chip swatches found at home improvement stores. Use a food safe brush to paint on cookie icing in three colors. You can use three different colors for a more striped effect, or you can use white icing to lighten a color into different shades for an ombré look. Mix your colors in a plastic cup or dish, adding more white to lighten each stripe.

Sparkling Sippers

Wet the rims of drinking glasses in a dish of clean water. Then dip the rims in a plate of colored sparkling sugar. Fill each glass with milk.

Crafts

Letter Art

For the first letter in each guest's first name, purchase large papier-mâché letters (available at craft stores). Supply different colors of yarn, craft glue, and embellishments. Apply glue in sections to one side of the letter, smoothing it out with an old paintbrush or your finger. Tightly wrap the yarn around in rows so that the letter doesn't show through. Keep wrapping until the entire letter is wrapped. When dry, add on embellishments. Girls now have new pieces of personal art for their rooms.

Li'l Letters

Celebrate your doll's name, too! Decorate a letter to hang in her space using chipboard letters sold in the scrap-book section of craft stores. If the letter is too little to easily wrap with yarn, cover it instead with patterned paper and stick on pretty embellishments.

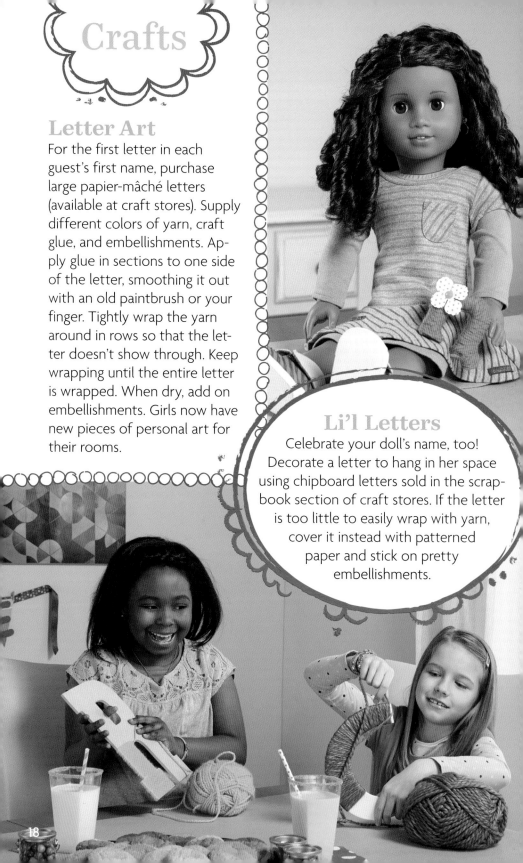

Painted Pillows

Create fun sayings on throw pillows for each of your guests' beds. Start by covering your work surface with a plastic tablecloth. Give each girl one white insert throw pillow (available at craft stores) and lay out adhesive-backed foam letters for each girl to spell out a word or phrase. Arrange and stick the letters onto the pillow. Cover the pillow with a fabric dye spray, using different colors to create a tie-dye effect. When dry, peel off the letters and send the pillows home to brighten up each girl's bed.

Doll Doodle

Guests can create mini masterpieces to display on their bulletin boards or framed on their nightstands. Punch out the doll doodle postcards from the back of the book and provide one to each girl. Using fine-point markers and colored pens, doodle repetitive patterns in the blank spaces to create a small piece of abstract art.

Good Clean Fun

Create games from your cleaning chores, and you'll probably want to do them more!

Sometimes all you need to do to change the look of your room is clean it up. Lurking under those stinky socks, scattered puzzle pieces, and cluttered shelves is a space that is ready to shine. Still, we know what you're thinking: Cleaning is boring! But doing your chores isn't a bore when you turn them into playtime. Give these activities a try when it's time to tidy up your room.

Animal Act

If you were an animal, how would your spruce up your space? Punch out the Animal Act cards from the back of the book and place them facedown in a pile. Mix them around and draw a card. Imagine how the animal on that card would clean: Does it hop? Walk on all fours? Wag its tail? Use their characteristics to clean!

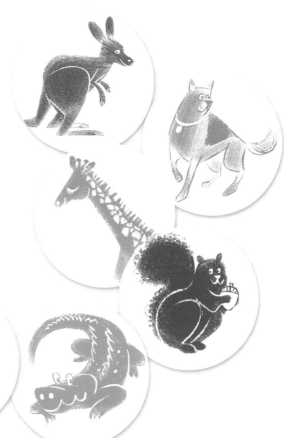

Color Code

Assemble the punch-out spinner from the back of the book and spin the arrow. The color it lands on is the color of the objects you need to clean in the room. For example, if the arrow points to pink, make your bed that has a pink comforter, throw your pink socks in the hamper, and reshelf that pink book you finished reading. When you complete all of one color, spin again until your room is colorfully clean!

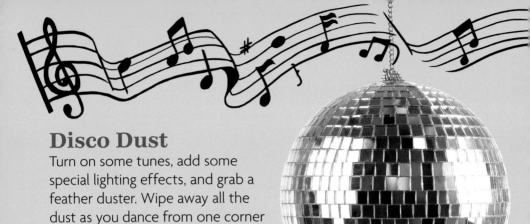

Disco Dust

Turn on some tunes, add some special lighting effects, and grab a feather duster. Wipe away all the dust as you dance from one corner to the other.

Play Hoops

Slam-dunk your dirty laundry into the hamper. Go into your closet for a few layups to put away your clean clothes. Toss crumpled paper into the wastebasket. Where do you have to stand in your room to make a 3-point shot?

Beat the Buzzer

Set a timer for 15 minutes. Challenge yourself to put everything in its place before the buzzer goes off.

Once Upon a Time

You have a masquerade ball to get to by 12 noon, but first you have to clean up your room! You'll save time if you dress for the ball before you begin. Don your craziest dress-up outfit or costume and start cleaning! If you don't finish by noon, your room will turn into a pumpkin. For extra credit, dress your doll up in her craziest outfit, too!

Set the Scene

Pretend that your room is a fancy boutique. Arrange and display everything nicely so that your customers will want to come back.

Messy Match-Up

When Mom says it's time to clean your room, challenge your siblings to see who can finish first. The winner gets to choose the games to play, things to do, and shows to watch for the rest of the day.

Room for Two?

Siblings sometimes have to share spaces, such as bedrooms, study spots, or playrooms, but that doesn't mean you can't have one that still feels like your own. Even if you love sports and the outdoors, and your sister is a total girly-girl, there are still ways to make the two styles work together for something you'll both love.

Step 1: List It

Tear out the duplicate worksheets in the back of the book, giving one to your sibling and keeping the other for yourself. Set a timer for about 10 minutes and complete each sheet on your own.

Step 2: Sort It

Review each of your lists together. Start by find-ing out what you both have in common. Use these favorites to pick a theme for your room.

Step 3: Make It Yours

So you both like the color blue, but your favorite shade is powder blue and your sister's favorite shade is royal blue. Instead of making all the details in the space the same shade of blue, use your favorite shades to help make it more personalized to you. It can also help to define whose bins are whose and how to keep your things separate, as well as neat and clean.

Step 4: Work It Out

If the two lists have absolutely nothing in common, you can still let each of your styles shine with a little compromising. For example, if you love soccer and the color green but your sister loves puppies and the color purple, find a way to meet in the middle. Find a poster of a puppy playing with a soccer ball to hang up. Or find accessories that combine purple and green. It's about creating a "together" zone that you will both like spending time in.

Step 5: Keep It Neat

Once you have the space you both love, work together to keep it clean and organized. When clutter begins to build up, make a chore list, assigning tasks to each person. Work together to help each other out and make the process easier.

Heads Up

Decorate your ceiling when the space below is all used up.

1. Open three wooden embroidery hoops in large, medium, and small. You'll use the inside piece of each.
2. Paint, decoupage, or cover large, medium, and small craft sticks in washi tape so that you have enough to fit around each hoop.
3. Using adhesive craft dots, attach the small sticks around the edges of the small hoop, the medium sticks around the edges of the medium hoop, and the large sticks around the edges of the large hoop.
4. Tie or duct-tape string at three equally spaced points on the small hoop, and tape to the inside of the medium craft sticks that it hangs below. Ask someone for help with holding, as it's easier to hang straight with two pairs of hands. Repeat with the medium hoop, attaching it to the inside of the large hoop.
5. Tie string at three points on the large hoop and hang from the ceiling.

Doll-Size Decor

Make a mini version to decorate your doll's space. Tape string at three points on the circular lid of a plastic container (don't worry how it looks, as the strings will be covered up). Decorate small craft sticks so that you have enough to fit around the entire lid. When dry, attach the sticks to the lip of the lid using adhesive craft dots. When completely covered, gather the strings and hang it in your doll's room.

Blooming Butterflies

✋ Let fluttering butterflies zoom around your room with this pretty paper craft. Using the butterfly stencil in the back, trace two shapes onto scrapbook paper. Cut out each shape and fold one piece in half, lengthwise. Apply double-sided adhesive tape to the fold and attach it to the center of the flat piece. Hang using removable wall-mounting tabs.

Decorate for Your Doll

Use the small size butterfly stencil to spruce up your doll's special space.

Paper Tape Pattern

When paint and wallpaper are too permanent for you, use washi tape to add some pizzazz to your space. Paper tape comes in all kinds of patterns, colors, and sizes, and removes easily without wrecking your walls. Create a cool zigzag pattern as a border, add stripes to a plain wall, or border your posters for a DIY-frame. Be creative!

Sweet Art

Sweeten up your walls with cute crafted cupcakes made from stacked pom-poms and baking liners. Use craft glue to secure one large pom-pom into a liner, and then glue a smaller pom-pom on top. Let dry. Hang by attaching removable wall-mounting tabs to the flat bottom of the liner and then sticking to the wall.

Poster Puzzle

A poster is an easy way to add art to your room, but if you want to make it look more modern, cut it up. 🖐️ Ask a parent to help you pick out some frames to use. They can be all the same size, or a mix of different sizes. Figure out how you want to lay out the frames by arranging them on the floor in a way that works with the shape of your poster. Use the frames as stencils to trace and cut out pieces of the poster. Put each piece in the frame and then ask a parent to help you hang them.

Petite Posters

Tear out the mini poster in the back, and make a doll-size version of this craft for her room. To frame each piece, use small craft sticks or cut strips of cardboard or card stock to tape together.

Zoned Out

When decorating, divide your room into zones— one area for each activity.

When your room feels like one big open box, decorating it can feel overwhelming. Try thinking of your room as a bunch of smaller spaces—or zones—and not only will it be easier to decorate, but it will also make the space you have more useful.

Sleep Zone

Where: Your bed.

Organize: To make sure you get a good night's sleep, try not to use your bed for other things such as doing homework or piling folded laundry.

Style: Where you catch your ZZZs is likely the biggest piece of furniture in your room. Use it to set your style by picking a quilt or comforter in a color or pattern you love. Or add in pops of color with pillow shams, stuffed animals, and throw pillows.

Craft: Tie-It T-Shirt Pillow
Turn old T-shirts into throw pillows. Cut a straight line across the top of the shirt and down each side. Cut fringe pieces around all edges. Knot front and back fringe pieces together on three sides. Stuff the pocket with batting or use a throw pillow insert. Tie off the last side of fringe, and display your new pillow on your bed.

Work Zone

Where: Your desk or tabletop area where you do your homework.

Organize: Be smart when studying by keeping your desk free of clutter. Display items that you use every day, and use drawers and bins to tuck away things you only need once in a while.

Style: Create pretty places to store your stuff, such as paper-wrapped cans, small boxes for erasers and paper clips, and patterned boxes for notepaper.

Craft: Homework Helper

Turn cereal or pasta boxes into a super storage caddy for your desk. Start by cutting the tops off three boxes of different sizes so that you have three different heights. Use invisible double-stick tape to stack the boxes together, with all the openings facing up. Decorate the boxes by covering them with different colors of duct tape. Place empty toilet paper rolls inside one box, cutting to fit if needed. This will help to keep your pens, pencils, and scissors separated.

Get-Ready Zone

Where: Near a mirror in your room, with a place to store jewelry and hair accessories.

Organize: Tidy up messy accessories with helpful hangers and cute containers.

Style: Turn a bold colored ice-cube tray into the perfect spot to keep small earrings, barrettes, and hair elastics. For longer hanging items, such as headbands, necklaces, and bracelets, use a bulletin board to dangle and display your jewelry.

Craft: Mane Attraction

Organize and display your hair tools and accessories at the same time. Create bright stripes by holding your hair elastics around the outside of a jar, vase, or drinking glass. Surround the rim with mini butterfly clips that are easy to grab when your hair needs a pinch. Use the container to hold your brush, comb, and hand mirror on top of your dresser.

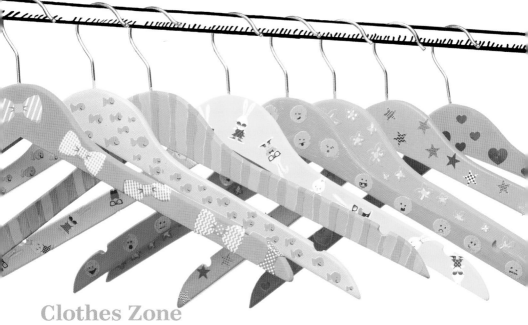

Clothes Zone

Where: Your clothes closet and dresser.

Use: There are four main ways to organize the clothing that hangs in your closet.

1. Season: Put last season's clothes at the back of the closet or in a bin under your bed.
2. Style: Hang all of your short-sleeved shirts together, then your button-down shirts, and then your sweaters and long-sleeved tees. Keep pants with pants and skirts with skirts.
3. Color: Keep reds and oranges at one end and blues and purples at the other. Mix and match outfits from the rainbow of colors.
4. Size: Hang your long pants and skirts on one end and your shorter skirts and shirts at the other end. Tuck a shoe rack in the open space beneath your shorter clothing.

Style: While there isn't much style you need to add to your closet—after all, it's behind closed doors—you can make it easier to style yourself and plan your outfits. Hang a canvas clothing organizer in your closet and label the compartments with days of the week. Pick out outfits and place them on the shelves, along with any accessories to wear or gear you need for the day.

Craft: Designer Hangers

Show off the clothes in your closet using decorated wooden hangers for tank tops, shirts, and dresses. On a covered surface, use acrylic paint and your favorite colors to create a pattern that is perfectly you. Let dry and embellish more if you'd like, before hanging in the closet.

Pal Presentation

Turn photos of your friends into dynamite displays!

The perfect artwork for your room can be pictures of you and your pals. Use these cute ideas and the punch-outs provided in the back to turn your friends' faces into works of art.

Pocket Pictures

Punch out the patterned paper from the back of the book and tape or glue school photos onto each. When dry, slide them into the pockets of a plastic trading-card sleeve. Tape on a ribbon or cord to the back of the sleeve to hang your pocket pictures.

Desk Display

⭐ Ask an adult to help you find a sheet of acrylic plastic (found at home improvement stores) to fit the top of your desk. Create a collage of patterned paper and photos, and arrange it on your desktop. Lay the plastic over the pictures for a pretty and practical display.

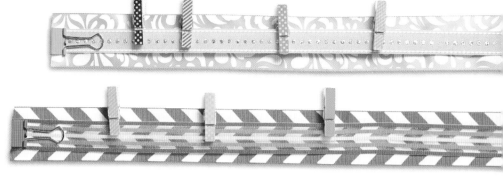

Ribbon Garland

Cut a length of wide ribbon and lay a coordinating narrow ribbon on top. Clip on decorative binder clips to hold the ribbons together at both ends. Use small wooden clothespins (available at craft stores) to attach photos to the thin ribbon.

Wall of Frame

Glass inserts can make frames look too formal. To keep your pics casual, just use the border. Collect mismatched frames in different colors, or paint each to help them pop. String a piece of baker's twine, using duct tape to secure the ends to the back of the frame. Use small wooden clothespins (available at craft stores) to hang one or more pictures on the line. Ask a parent to help you hang your frames to make a cool collection on your wall.

Better with Boxes

Turn boxes into decor that's so much more than just shoe storage.

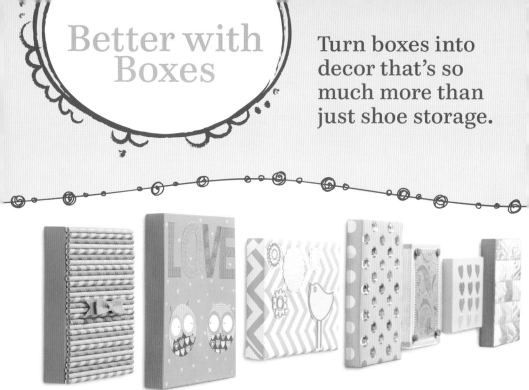

Awesome Art

Use shoebox tops as the perfect blank canvas for your art. Paint them solid colors, and then when dry, use stencils to spell out your name. Or cover with old maps and make a cool memento by adding photos and postcards from a favorite vacation. Stickers, scrapbook supplies, and little objects from around your room can all easily become art. Just use your imagination!

Darling Display

Paint the inside and outside of a shoebox in two different colors. Once dry, ask an adult to help you hang it on the wall. Use your new shelf to show off your favorite lightweight items.

Cubby Cute

Skip the fabric bins you can get at the store, and keep your room nice and neat with spruced-up shoeboxes instead. Wrap shoebox bottoms in decorative wrapping papers. Tape the ends of the paper inside the boxes to keep the outsides nice and neat. Store in a cubby or on a shelf with the punch-out labels from the back of the book.

Ribbon Wrangler

Whether you use ribbon to spice up your crafts or add a pop of color to your ponytail, you know what a tangled mess the spools can make. Keep your ribbons from running wild by transforming a small shoebox into a ribbon organizer. Using a large handheld hole-punch, punch openings along the two long sides of a plain or decorated box, about two inches apart. Place the ribbon spools inside the box on their sides and string each ribbon through a hole from the inside of the box. When you need a piece, simply pull and cut, leaving a little tail peeking through.

Just for Jewelry

Paint or cover a box top with decorative paper or fabric. When dry, stick on adhesive-backed hooks to one edge of the lid or ask a parent to screw in teacup hooks. Hang on the wall, and use the hooks to keep your jewelry from getting tangled.

From Box to Basket

Make a box look more like a basket by wrapping it in thick yarn. Use craft glue to help the yarn stick to the box. Add the glue as you go instead of all at one time. If needed, use removable tape to help hold the yarn in place until the glue dries.

Space Solutions

Got a problem with your space? There's room to fix it!

It can be hard to make way for a stylish space when your room is full of decorating roadblocks. Don't worry! We can help you find your way.

Color Clash

Whether your room is plain white or a shade that is simply not your fave, colors are a common conundrum when decorating. The obvious way is to ask your parents for permission to repaint your room. If they give the OK, choose a color carefully, as it'll likely be a while before you get to paint your room again. Or, try these no-paint solutions instead:

Add large art. Create a cool picture collage on one large wall. Instead of the wall color you dislike being the focal point, your eye will be drawn to your DIY art.

Accessorize. Pillows, lamps, frames, and rugs in a color that complements your walls can completely change the look.

Curtain call. Ask a parent to help you hang a rod with two curtains in a fun pattern or bold color behind or in place of your headboard. It will cover the wall, masking the color, and create a dramatic statement piece.

Baby Blues

If your room makes you feel more like a toddler than a tween, then it's time to make it more age appropriate. Add other colors in your room using accessories to help tone down pastel pink and soft butter yellow walls. Get permission to hang up posters that reflect your personal style. If your bedspread is too cartoony, flip it over to show the solid side instead.

Tiny Territory

If your room feels like the walls are closing in on you, try these ideas for more space:

Hang mirrors. You might not be able to change the square footage of your space, but you can trick the eye. Mirrors help to reflect more light, making the room seem bigger.

Shift your stuff. If your bed is right in the middle of your room, you might be able to create more space by pushing it up against the wall.

Lighten up. Dark decor can make a room feel smaller than it really is. Keep curtains, rugs, and bedspreads in light colors and lightweight fabrics.

Crowded Quarters

If there is stuff everywhere in your room, cleaning might not be enough of a space-solving solution. Go through the items in your room and create three piles: Keep, Toss, and Donate. Sort your stuff into these groups, making sure to ask yourself what you really need and use. If there is something that has sentimental value but you don't necessarily need it, store it somewhere out of the way for safekeeping.

Send your room ideas to
Styling Spaces **Editor**
American Girl
8400 Fairway Place
Middleton, WI 53562

(Sorry, but photos can't be returned. All comments
and suggestions received by American Girl may be
used without compensation or acknowledgment.)

Here are some other American Girl books you might like:

Each sold separately. Find more books online at americangirl.com.

CAN'T talk right meow come back in a bit!

American Cat
9 LIVES TO ENJOY
10 FUNNY JOKES

CAN'T talk right meow come back in a bit!

American Cat
9 LIVES TO ENJOY
10 FUNNY JOKES

©/™ 2016 American Girl

©/™ 2016 American Girl

©/™ 2016 American Girl

©/™ 2016 American Girl

©/™ 2016 American Girl

©/™ 2016 American Girl

truly me

INSTRUCTIONS:

1. Punch out the wheel and spinner.
2. Punch out the center hole in the wheel.
3. Place the wheel color-side up.
4. Punch out the spinner's tabs and fold them under.
5. Push the tabs through the wheel's hole and flatten them out so the spinner stays in place.
6. Place the color wheel on a hard surface to spin.

Room for Two?

1. Rank each color, with 1 being your favorite and 7 being your least favorite.

_____ _____ _____ _____ _____ _____ _____

2. Circle your three favorite animals.

3. Circle your three favorite activities:

4. List five things you love about your room as it is.

_____

_____

5. List five things you dislike about your room as it is.

_____

_____

6. What's the one thing in your room that you couldn't live without?

_____

_____

Room for Two?

Worksheet to accompany page 24.

1. Rank each color, with 1 being your favorite and 7 being your least favorite.

2. Circle your three favorite animals.

3. Circle your three favorite activities:

4. List five things you love about your room as it is.

_____

_____

5. List five things you dislike about your room as it is.

_____

_____

6. What's the one thing in your room that you couldn't live without?

_____

_____

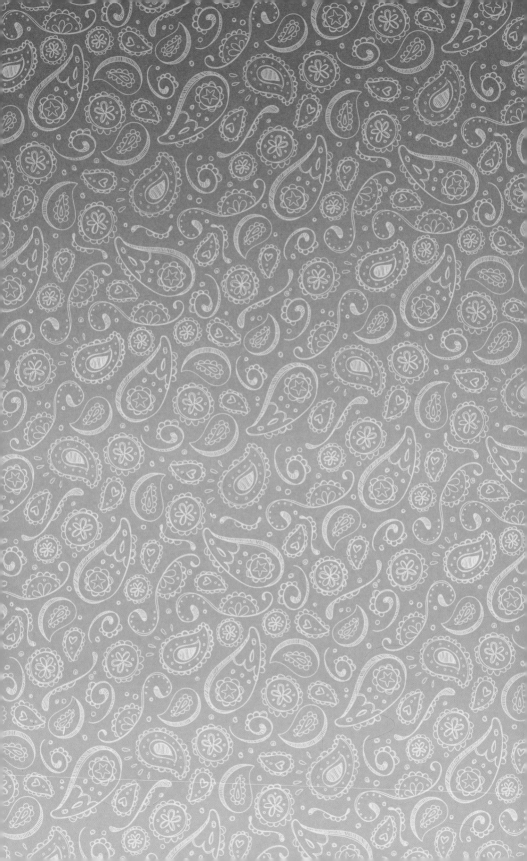

photos

toys

crafts

jewelry

cards

hair

misc.

crafts

photos

hair